Using Drills
in English Language Teaching

Tony Penston

tp TP Publications

TP Publications
59 Applewood Heights
Greystones
Co. Wicklow
Ireland

www.tppublications.com

© Tony Penston 2021

First published 2021

ISBN: 978 0 9531323 6 2

All rights reserved. No part of this publication may be reproduced, stored in a retrieval system or transmitted in any form or by any means without the prior written permission of the copyright owner or unless as expressly permitted by law, by licence or under terms agreed with the appropriate reprographics rights organization.

Links to third party websites are provided by TP Publications (TPP) in good faith and for information only. TPP disclaims any responsibility for the materials contained in any third party website referenced in this work.

Cover creation by Kevin Brooks
Cover background: Cardsuprint Ltd
Drawings by the author

Printed by Ross Print, Greystones, Ireland

Thanks

We are very grateful to the following for their comments and suggestions: Rose Aylett, freelance CELTA tutor, Liverpool; Rafaela Bepe of Lanna International School, Chiang Mai; Eamonn Coghlan of Altamont English, Westport; Dana Jalinkova, freelance teacher/trainer, Prague; Mariana Laxague of L'albero di Antonia School, Turin; Dermot McSharry of Swan English Language Training, Dublin; Joanna Morrison Jones of British School Pisa; Lianne Pavlíková, freelance teacher, Prievidza, Slovakia; Chiara Rizzo of International House Milan.
Special thanks to Wayne Rimmer for his generous assistance and expert advice.
Special thanks to Scott Thornbury for his insights and recommendations for further reading on frequency effects in language learning.
Special thanks to Monique Walsh and Harish Verma of ELTA, Dublin, for their information on the Callan Method, for which their school is renowned.

Acknowledgements

We are grateful to the following for their kind permission to reproduce copyright material: p7 Macmillan Publishers; p8 Oxford University Press; pp19, 30 Cambridge University Press; p20 Hancock McDonald; p21 DepositPhotos (adjusted); p34 National Geographic Learning.

The publishers have made every effort to trace and acknowledge copyright holders. If, however, they have inadvertently overlooked any they will be pleased to make the necessary arrangements at the first opportunity.

Abbreviations and terminology

CLT: Communicative Language Teaching
ELT: English Language Teaching
S: Student   Ss: Students   T: Teacher   T-S: Teacher to student, and vice versa.
(): a pause in a dialogue/conversaton
The words *student* and *learner* are used with author preference for their context.
The word *sentence* when used in drilling is to mean a short sentence, a clause or phrase.
The use of phonemes is kept to a minimum, in keeping with the informal language preferred in this book.

Tony Penston has taught English and trained teachers of English for more years than he cares to remember. He now shares his time between occasional teaching, examining and writing, not neglecting his musical and other interests. His other publications include *A Concise Grammar for English Language Teachers, Essential Phonetics for English Language Teachers, A History of Ireland for Learners of English,* and the poster, *The Articulation of Difficult Consonants.*

Preface

These days there are *How to…* books for everything, including of course everything concerning English language teaching, *How to Teach Grammar, How to Teach Pronunciation, How to Teach Vocabulary, How to Teach Speaking*. Along with these just about every other aspect of language teaching is covered in various publications.

So why, prior to this, has there been no publication on Drilling in English language teaching? Most if not all methodology books have a section on drilling, and when we know that 'repeat' is a common command of language teachers then we would expect some guidebook to be available. I could surmise that there is still some unease about promoting drilling, accountable by its association with 'parroting', the meaningless repetition exacted in rote learning. While lately there has been some renewed interest in drilling, there appears to be a lack of concord regarding the types of drills, the suitability of text for repetition, but most importantly, how the use of drills should conform to principles of communicative language teaching (CLT).

The stimuli for writing this booklet were 1) the fact that I believe strongly in the value of drilling and wished to present a review of and rationale for its use, with coherent and practical guidelines for its implementation, 2) my desire to explain how drilling, a non-communicative activity, can be accommodated in the communicative approach to language teaching by grafting principles of Immersion Learning onto those of CLT.

This book is not a compendium of intensive speaking activities – the reader can easily access such online or in bookstores. The intention is to guide the teacher in prioritising context and maintaining learner-centredness even in simple repetition. Activities there are, of course, but these are maintained at a relatively small number to serve as examples and to ensure that this book remains affordable.

As with my other publications I've not restricted myself, I hope, to a narrow treatment of the topic (grammar, phonetics) but try to offer advice within a holistic approach to teaching, hence my references to different stages of a typical lesson, and the provision of a lesson plan format (Appendix). There is also regard for teaching different age groups and teaching online.

I recommend the use of coursebooks in language teaching. Reputable publishers and authors can be relied upon to create attractive material within reliable syllabi. In each lesson and in the accompanying workbooks there are normally sections on controlled practice, and I pay particular attention to how such practice can be directed, with drilling.

In explaining most pronunciation errors I have avoided using phonemes for simplicity's sake. If readers seek a more precise treatment I would direct them to *Essential Phonetics for English Language Teachers*.

Comments and suggestions from readers are always welcome:
info@tppublications.com

Contents

Preface 4

PART 1
Background and rationale

The audio-lingual method 6
The communicative approach 9
Bad drilling 11
Drilling and the communicative approach 13
Seven reasons for drilling 14
Sound patterns 16
In summary 17

PART 2
Drilling in practice

Good drilling 18
WB work 24
When to choral drill 27
Controlled Practice 28
Drilling a sentence on the WB 31
Other activities:
  1 Short dialogues 33
  2 Video 35
  3 Poetry 35
  4 Jazz chants® 38
  5 Songs 40
  6 Limericks 40
  7 Disappearing text 41
  8 Chaining 42
  9 Role-play 43
Conclusion and outlook 44

Appendix – Lesson plan format 45
Dictogloss – The Claddagh Ring 46

PART 1
Background and rationale

Rote learning, prior to a 'method'

For centuries, language teaching and learning has been done (or had been done, depending on your perspective) by rote learning, repetition, practice. As demand grew, a 'method' developed, a procedure to be followed class by class, based on current beliefs.

The audio-lingual method

The audio-lingual method of language teaching (though it may not have had that name then) was developed originally for the American military in the 1940s, and was later adopted by many institutes. Its rationale is based on Behaviorism, a theory which holds that we learn most things by practice and habit formation. Do we learn a new language by practice and habit formation? B.F. Skinner (1957) claimed that we could.

Each lesson consisted of a dialogue – read aloud by the teacher and repeated line by line by the students (Ss) – followed by a brief grammar explanation, then more repetition (drilling), in the classroom and later in the newly invented language laboratory. The use of L1 was strictly forbidden.

It wouldn't be worthwhile here examining the range of drills proposed then; they number seven in Larsen-Freeman (1986) and over ten in Richards and Rodgers (1986) quoting Brooks (1964). However, besides the straight-forward Repetition, here are two:

1. Transformation drill

Ss change the form of a sentence from positive to negative, from statement to question, etc, e.g.

> T: He knows my address.
> Ss: He doesn't know my address.
> T: They go shopping every day.
> Ss: They don't go shopping every day.

2. Substitution drill

The teacher says a line, then a word or a phrase (the cue). The students repeat the line (the response) with the cue and any changes necessary, e.g.

T: Every day John goes sailing. Yesterday.
Ss: Yesterday John went sailing.
T: Every day John goes sailing. We.
Ss: Every day we go sailing.

The excerpt below from *New English 900* (Collier Macmillan) shows a variation of the substitution drill. In this once popular American publication none of the cues require a change in the model sentence/pattern, though some of the cued pronouns under sentence 2 in this exercise would seem to require that the fixed first or second person pronoun in the subordinate clause be altered to correspond.

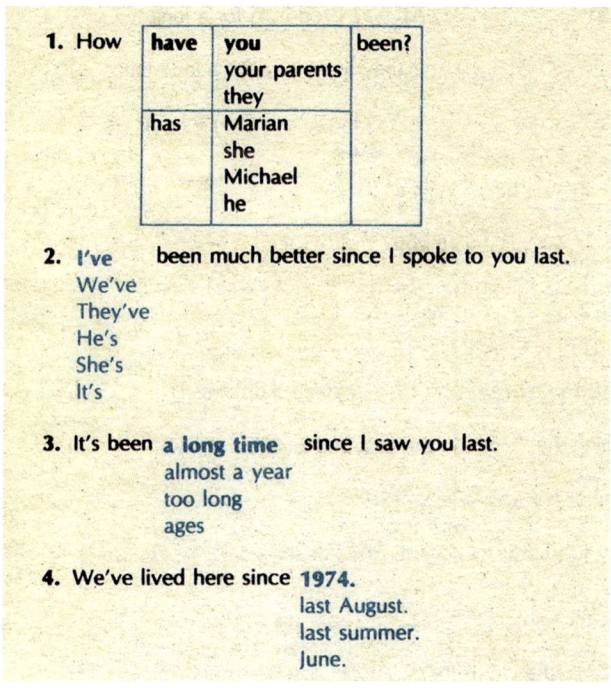

Figure 1 Grammar table and substitution drills, from *New English 900* (1978, based on 1964 edn.)

Below is an excerpt from *A Practical English Grammar – Structure Drills 2* (Thomson & Martinet). In this once popular British publication most of the drills (20 per exercise) are situation-based and consist of a two-line dialogue. Some thought is occasionally required in forming the second line, a small move away from 'parrotting'. The methodology was known as **structural-situational**, variations of which were in use from the 50s.

> (a) A: Someone will have to get maps.
>   B: *Yes. Would you mind getting them?* (slight stress on **you**)
>
> (b) A: Someone will have to put the milk bottles out.
>   B: Yes. *Would you mind putting them out?* (Notice word order.) (slight stress on **you**)
>
> *Someone will have to . . .*
> 1 make sandwiches.
> 2 fill the thermoses.
> 3 keep an eye on the children.
> 4 buy maps.
> 5 work out our route. (*See* (b) *above.*)
> 6 pick up the traveller's cheques. (*See* (b) *above.*)
> 7 book the rooms.

Figure 2   From *Structure Drills 2* (Oxford University Press 1979)

Moving on, with a look back

There is no need to evaluate any of the drills above, enough to say that they would not be seen, at least in those formats, in any modern coursebook or workbook. However, the germ of many mini-dialogues for practice in modern lessons is visible in structural-situational lessons as exemplified above. Here is one from a modern English coursebook:

> a Complete the conversations with *will / shall* or *be going to* and the correct form of the verb.
>
>   1 A Could you take the rubbish out? It's beginning to smell.
>   B I _____ it as soon as this programme finishes. (do)
>   2 A _____ you _____ that pasta? You've hardly eaten any. (finish)
>   B I can't, I'm just not hungry. But don't throw it away. I _____ it for lunch tomorrow. (have)
>   3 A Don't put bottles in the black bin. You need to put them in the recycling bin.
>   B Sorry, I forgot. I _____ it again. (not do)
>   4 A This lasagne's been in the fridge for three days. _____ I _____ it away? (throw)
>   B No, don't waste it. Put it in the freezer.

Figure 2   From *English File 4ᵗʰ ed. Intermediate Plus* (Oxford University Press 2019)

The Communicative Approach

The late 1970's and early 80's saw the emergence of works such as *Teaching Language as Communication* (Widdowson) and *Communicative Language Teaching* (Littlewood), which contained explanatory chapters and suggested activities such as information-gap (student A has a map with some differences from student B's; both students must agree the best route without looking at each other's maps) and role-play, giving teachers and coursebook writers the means with which to generate S-S (student-to-student) communication in the classroom. This approach, rather than a methodology, became known as the Communicative Approach to Language Teaching/Learning.

Coinciding with arguments in favour of more communication in language teaching, the Council of Europe produced a syllabus not based on grammar but on language functions (Van Ek and Alexander, 1977). The format graduated to 'can do' statements, on which the Council of Europe Framework of Reference for Languages: Learning, Teaching, Assessment (CEFR) is based.

Emphasis on meaning – neglect of drilling

With the Communicative Approach the focus of learning shifted from repetition to meaningful interaction. The reading and listening inputs in coursebook lessons were more relevant, and the set pairwork activities generated more S-S speaking; however, intensive oral practice was lacking, especially for those whose L1 was very different from English. Over time, methods like The Callan Method* and fads like Crazy English (developed by Li Yang in China and reaching its height in 2008, entailing large groups of students shouting repetitions) grew to answer the demand for intensive repetition in their own ways. Accusations of 'throwing the baby out with the bathwater' were heard from educators who lamented that drilling was being neglected in contemporary coursebooks.

*The Callan Method, in existence from the 60s, consists of introductory choral repetition, then T-S question-and-answer, with instant correction. The teacher repeats each question before 'shadow answering' with the student and correcting any pronunciation errors. The lesson is normally repeated as homework (with audio input) and the following day's lesson consists of a review of that lesson followed by new material. The method was preceded by the Direct Method, still also in use, a method concentrating similarly on oral work but not in such an intensive question-and-answer way.

Lexis, and back to 'pattern'

The Lexical Approach by M. Lewis (1993) advocated a greater focus on lexis, and as corpus linguistics enabled us to see definitively how groups of the same words commonly occurred, the term *chunks* (similar to *collocation*) was invented to refer to them. So now we could say that we have lexical *chunks* and grammatical *patterns*. Where practicality is concerned the difference between *chunk* and *pattern* is hardly important; what is important is that we agree that **the ability to store groups of words in memory and produce them fluently and appropriately is largely dependent on repetition – repetition with meaning.**

Patterns in corpora

Corpora such as the Corpus of Contemporary American English (COCA), which contains over 1 billion words of written and spoken text, can provide information on frequency of words and phrases, collocation, etc. For example, if you wanted to know which pattern was more frequently used, *came up with the idea of* + -ing form or *came up with the idea to* (+ verb), you would arrive at the result below, which may influence your teaching/drilling of such patterns. It may also ignite or build your interest in the choice between infinitive or –ing form when either is grammatically acceptable; see Penston (2005) p97.

Example	COCA frequency (of the pattern in italics)
Dan *came up with the idea of* collecting food for the needy in New York.	158
Wilson… *came up with the idea to* use the turkey leg as a microphone. (Eliza Murphy, ABC News blog, 2012)	73

Figure 3 Selections and data from COCA. The top example is a little altered (I know the Dan in New York).

Are we there yet?

There may yet be arguments in favour of substitution drills and other non-simple repetition, especially when used for intensive pronunciation practice. However, the reason for my eschewing them or at least cautioning against them, and why you'll hardly find them in modern coursebooks, is that they place low priority on context, and **context is key in real communicative language teaching**. There follow three examples of bad drilling.

Bad drilling 1: person not identified

Here is an example of a substitution drill found recently on an ELT site (students' supposed lines inserted):

> Teacher: She has gone to the movies. Repeat.
> Students: She has gone to the movies.
> T: The park. She has gone...
> Ss: She has gone to the park.
> T: They.
> Ss: They has... They have gone to the park.

In order for the above to have value the students should know the identity of 'she', and whether it's the same 'she' who has gone to two separate places, the movie and the park, and if so, why. Similarly with 'they', etc. Such matters of context did not merit consideration in the audio-lingual days but should now. Would today's teacher have the time and inclination to create viable context?

Bad drilling 2: little or no coherence

Here is an example taken from a popular teacher's site at time of publication. It is listed as an example of a substitution drill, but not explicity advocated for teaching;

> T: I have a new car.
> Ss: Have you?
> T: I don't like fish.
> Ss: Don't you?
> T: I love coffee.
> Ss: Do you?

The announcement of having changed cars would well warrant a surprise/interest question. However, it's not terribly unusual for some people to dislike fish, certainly to love coffee, so the response, in the form of a reduced question, is forced here, lacking in coherence, with the danger that students, through mechanically answering with the given structure, would unlearn the meaning value of the question (or distrust the teacher's choice of examples).

Meaning, not structure, should be the driver of the language. More information (e.g. *I'm Japanese, I don't like fish*) or different items in the cue would be needed to elicit the surprise/interest question, for example:

> T: I don't like ice cream.
> Ss: Don't you?
> T: I love sour milk.
> Ss: Do you?

However, even with more realistic cue-responses, the series of disconnected interactions, common to most audio-lingual drills, seriously conflicts with rules of coherence and consequently principles of communicative language teaching. Incorporating a small number of such interactions into a decent dialogue would result in more enjoyment (for teacher and learner) and more retention, and that's how one would expect to find them in a modern coursebook.

Litmus test

Before presenting an example of targeted language for repetition, a teacher should ask themselves, "Would I say this in this situation?" and if the answer is "no", even "perhaps not, but…" it should be jettisoned. If still in doubt, a search in a corpus such as the Corpus of Contemporary American English will help out; if the pattern in question has an exceptionally low or zero frequency, drop it. Never compromise on accepted usage.

Bad drilling 3: change of intonation, stress or volume without reason

This was not suggested in audio-lingual methodology but seems to have come into use relatively recently. Students are asked to repeat (again) the same sentence but with a different intonation or stress pattern or at a different volume ("Now say it in a sad voice."), the cited reason being to avoid boredom while extending the practice.

Alternative intonation and contrastive stress must of course be part of the ELT syllabus, but these would normally be part of a particular lesson. For example:

Alternative intonation:
> Identify which of the below intonation lines belongs to an enthusing dog owner and which to the suspicious dog:

Figure 4 Intonation lines. The bottom one, low to low rise, is assumed to be the dog's.

Contrastive stress:

1. Put a stress mark above the word in sentence A to distinguish the place, and above the word in sentence B to distinguish the person.
2. Can you think of a context for each sentence?

   A This is where I come in.

   B This is where I come in.

Answers: 1. *This* in sentence A and *I* in sentence B.
2. In A, an actor during rehearsals, indicating and emphasising the location of their stage entry; in B, a participant at a planning meeting, about to explain their upcoming role.

If not a planned part of a lesson such language work can easily emerge within it, and in either case full context would be clear. For all other drills, retain the context in which the sentence has been first presented, and if boredom threatens, move on.

In real communication we don't vary intonation, stress or volume for no obvious reason. With children there is an exception, because kids are still experimenting with sounds and will readily cooperate in changing volume, whispering, speeding up, mumbling, once instructed with the enthusiasm that teachers of young learners usually possess and impart.

Drilling and the communicative approach

How can drilling be accommodated in the communicative approach? The answer to this question can be found by observing immersion learning in action. Children learning their first language (L1) especially, and others learning an L2 by total immersion, use repetition freely in their endeavours. And no one tells them to stop because they are not following the communicative approach. One crucial factor in their repetition is that **the concept is constantly held throughout** – no substitute words, no transformations, change of intonation, etc.

I have formulated **Immersion Learning Principles** (forthcoming) which can be used as guidelines in understanding and implementing 'real' communicative language teaching. The principles regarding repetition were born of the first three observations below.

Seven reasons for drilling

1. It's part of L1 immersion learning
The bulk of children's L1 learning is done through repetition. Children ask to hear the same stories again and again. They love role-play and will replay the same scene often. Some of them will repeat the last few words of your utterances just for the fun of it. Children are programmed to learn, and the program is perfectly designed. Adults learn a lot differently from children, but certain learning mechanisms stay with us, especially the one of repetition as practice.

2. It's part of L2 immersion learning
When you are abroad and you look up a phrase in your translator app or booklet, **do you repeat it to yourself before using it?** This is the 'getting your tongue around it' practice, the real 'habit learning' that we instinctively value. (Of course you can use a voice translator app, but where's the fun in that, or the appreciation for the effort you've made?)

3. There are learners who like it
Have you observed that **good language learners have few inhibitions**? A Turkish waiter, after having me put a sentence into better English for him, went about his work repeating the sentence at least eight times. This is not to say that uninhibited repetition is essential for learning, just that those who like to repeat should be given the opportunity to do so.

4. Learners commonly ask for more 'speaking'
New students in language schools commonly tick 'more speaking' when filling in their needs analysis form. Teachers often interpret this as a request for more discussion, role-play etc, being unaware of the fact that drilling is an aspect of 'speaking', and that very many students understand the value of it.

5. Choral drilling builds confidence
Ss who would be diffident about speaking in class may gain confidence on hearing their peers repeat a model sentence. Such students have been noted to participate on the second or third repetition; but participate or no, hearing a sentence spoken well a number of times is beneficial for all.

6. It consolidates the motor skill of articulation

When learning new L2 language sounds, students should be taught to feel the articulations involved, i.e. what's happening mainly with their lips and tongue (see Underhill 2018a). But then the new sounds have to be automatized in fluent speech, and this can only be done by repetition.

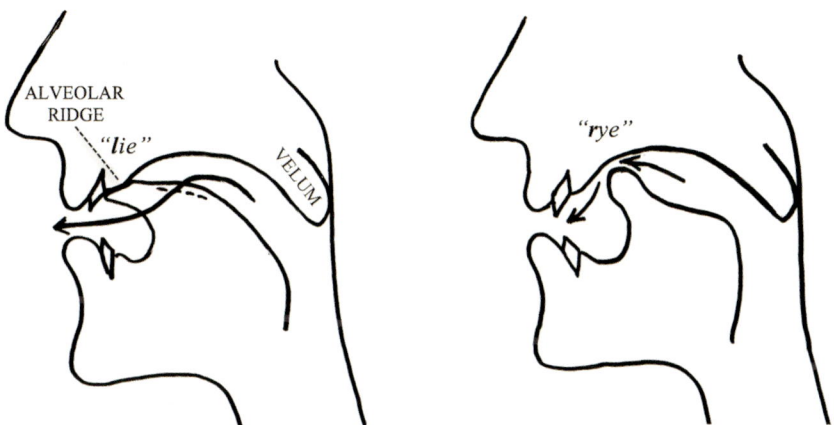

Figure 5 Articulation of /l/ and /r/, from *Essential Phonetics for English Language Teachers* (Penston 2015)

7. We really do learn by practice

Behaviorism, the theory of learning set out by B.F. Skinner and commonly accepted as the rationale for the audio-lingual method, says, in a nutshell, **we learn by practice**, by noting and trying to produce a pattern correctly (and being rewarded for this) and by repeating it, habitualizing it. This is how you learned to hold your knife and fork (or chopsticks), to ride a bike, drive a car, to play a musical instrument, and yes, to pronounce and put language sounds together.

The above advocacy of repetition is put more academically of course by experts such as Nick C. Ellis in 'Frequency effects in language processing' (2002).

And we should say here that *iteration* would be more precise than *repetition* to describe what's happening when Ss repeat again, because learners don't repeat the same pattern as an exact replica, rather there is a slight improvement, in most cases, with each iteration/repetition, as the listening and motor skills sharpen. (Thanks to Adrian Underhill for this point.) Repetition alone was how I was taught my arithmetic tables – no iteration, and little cognition, applying there.

Sound patterns

Have you ever noticed how you can continue humming a tune if it stops abruptly? But more remarkably, have you noticed how you can 'hear' and start humming the next track on an often-played album before it starts?. This is an interesting case of memory of audio pattern only. This does not contradict what we say about the importance of meaning with repetition: meaning is paramount, it is essential for accessing language items from memory (and storing them there); however, sound pattern also plays a part, and helps maintain the flow of language, as it does the flow of music. The retention of musical pattern reminds us of the importance of prosody (stress, rhythm, intonation) when we are teaching the speaking skill.

An interesting example of 'tight' collocation or chunking is how we can instantly predict the next word in "He was refused planning _____" (permission). This pattern carries plenty of meaning. Now look at this: "Hickory Dickory ____." Again we can instantly slot in the missing word, yet this pattern carries no meaning, it is a sound pattern only. How much a sound pattern assists the learning of a meaningful pattern may not be known, but the empirical evidence of the connection between both is around us every day.

Still on sound, but perhaps with some attention to meaning, have you ever had to memorize the lyrics of a song? Did singing it aloud help? This is not a completely rhetorical question – some people learn by 'hearing' the words and music deeply, subvocalising, listening to themselves. Some may need the duality of meaning with sound, others will prioritize sound, inventing words or phrases, sometimes nonsense ones, to replace ones they can't 'catch', in order to retain the rhythm.

Children often amuse and sometimes astound us by coming out with common utterances of a parent/minder, without apparently having practised them. Hearing the same pattern a number of times (while noting its meaning), without overtly practising it, obviously helps learning.

Quiet students may opt out

It seems that observations of learning taking place mainly by listening, as exemplified above, would lend support to the argument that quiet students should be allowed to maintain low participation during drilling routines. I believe this is acceptable under certain conditions:
1. The student has unambiguously shown or stated their desire to opt out of the drilling.

2 The student is actively listening during drilling, proved by their demeanour and by providing correct short answers occasionally. Allied to this is subvocalising, imperceptibly moving speech articulators (tongue, lips, velum, larynx…), occasionally done while quietly reading, but probably also done by a quiet student during a drilling session.
3 The student's pronunciation is not poor (not requiring much 'get your tongue round it' practice).
4 The student participates in other speaking activities (pair work, language games) normally.

If any of these conditions is not observed, the teacher or line manager should have a respectful talk with the student to ascertain the reason for their reticence. Of course the choice is ultimately with the student, in a learner-centred environment.

Let students listen before repeating

Related to sound patterns and some Ss preferring to just listen, above, there is a belief that we shouldn't have students repeat immediately after we provide the model. Underhill (2018b) recommends that students be first invited to listen to the model *'internally, using their own inner ear. This internal replay can catch qualities of the original pronunciation that get lost if repeated aloud immediately'*. The teacher may then provide the model again before asking for a repetition. This technique may be 'grafted' easily onto the typical method of drilling outlined in this book; however, it may be suited more to a dedicated pronunciation lesson with a monolingual L1 group rather than to individual error correction especially with a mixed L1 group.

In summary

The communicative approach put an end to meaningless drilling, but so far, the place or manner of drilling within its guidelines remains unclear, By observing learners in immersion situations we can be sure of the value of including meaningful drilling in our teaching, aided by the 'concept is key' maxim.

Where difficulty with specific sounds is concerned, we should help by teaching articulations, using static images or/and MRI video clips (on Youtube, e.g.)

Finally, we must be aware that repetitious listening may be as effective as repetitious speaking for some learners, and more research into this would be welcomed.

PART 2
Drilling in practice

Simple, straight-forward repetition
Today, thankfully, most audio-lingual drills have been consigned to the ELT archive. When teachers drill they tend to use simple repetition of the sentence or phrase which is being met in context, or whose credible context can be imagined if the sentence is in an exercise list. This is apart from specific pronunciation lessons which might involve a list of words and even some substitution drills; nevertheless, it behoves the teacher to provide context wherever it may be lacking.

Good drilling

At the outset
First of all ensure that your students understand the benefits of repetition. At lower levels and especially for students whose L1 has greatly different phonology from English this is normally a given. You may be surprised by the positive reaction to drilling. Not many teachers approach repetition as a viable 'speaking' activity, but in contrast I have found that many students do.

After correcting the word, drill the phrase
Much correction in advance of drilling centres on one, sometimes two, words occurring in a sentence. When a word is mispronounced its correct version may be repeated once or twice, but a drilling of the phrase or/and clause in which it occurs within the lesson should follow, thus providing practice with the rhythmical and structural patterns of English and assisting in memory retention.

Keep it alive
In a pronunciation lesson, lists of words, e.g. minimal pairs, may be drilled for phonemic discrimination practice, e.g. *ship* and *sheep*, *parrot* and *palate*, *rope* and *robe*, etc, but it's good to include a little communicative interaction along the way, e.g. when a check reveals a difficulty:

2 Minimal pairs

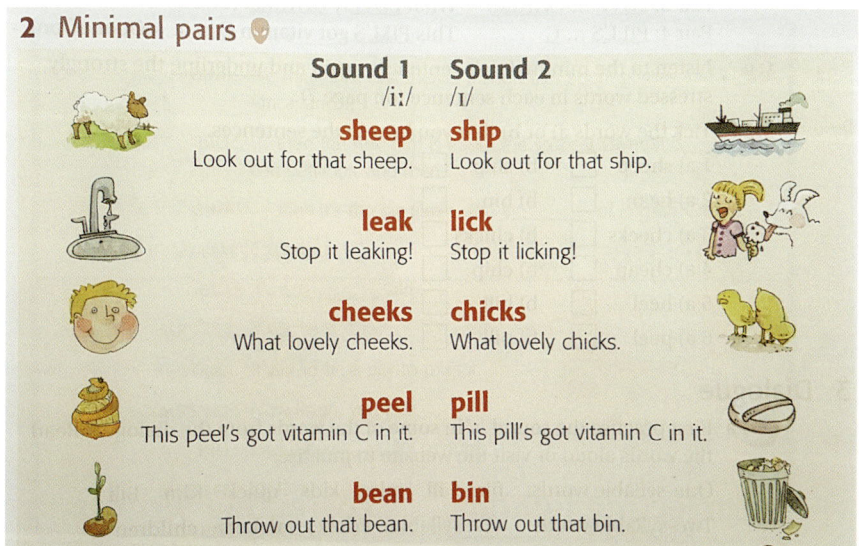

Figure 5 From *Ship or Sheep* by Ann Baker (Cambridge University Press 2006)
Reproduced with permission of the Licensor through PLSClear

[() = a pause. Underlined words are spoken prominently]
T: By the way, Carlos, what kind of bins do you have in your home?
C: Black beans, green beans…
T: Interesting, thanks, so you like black <u>beans</u> (mimes eating, or highlights the drawing of a bean in the list of minimal pairs on the WB). But I meant rubbish <u>bins</u>, like this one, (highlights drawing of bin in the minimal pairs list, or/and points to one in the classroom or shows one online), <u>bins</u>, ugh (taps the bin image), not <u>beans</u>, yum, yum (taps the bean image) (Carlos and class laugh).
() Ok, everyone listen and repeat (mimes eating): black <u>beans</u> (Ss repeat).
(Points to bin) Rubbish <u>bins</u> (Ss repeat). (Drill once more.)
() Do you have pedal bins (demonstrating with foot in classroom or showing one online), or … What kind of <u>bins</u> to you have at home? (Carlos answers.) Good, thank you Carlos. Now, (nominating one more student to relieve Carlos) Laila, ask <u>me</u> the question, What kind of… (pointing to bin)… etc.
(Wheelie bin should enter the interaction somewhere. Coincidentally, those two words have the *sheep* and *ship* vowels.)

Figure 6 From *Pronpack 3: Pronunciation Pairworks* by Mark Hancock (2017). Minimal pairs in phrases.

Backchaining / Backward build-up

Backchaining or backward build-up is the term used for starting the drill from the end of the sentence. It is usually only required if the string is long (the suggested maximum is six stresses), with students trailing off or getting out of sync towards the end, or if the final words are difficult to pronounce. In the following example the students' repetitions are omitted. The teacher would highlight the corresponding parts of the sentence on the WB.

> T: their mistakes.
> T: everyone gives to their mistakes.
> T: the name everyone gives to their mistakes.
> T: Experience is the name everyone gives to their mistakes.

Alternatively, the above sentence can be drilled in two (or more) separate parts, e.g. *Experience is the name* followed by *everyone gives to their mistakes*, and these then joined together. Or again, front-chaining can be used, i.e. the reverse of backchaining. Backchaining would be the most advisable, because it's normally the end of the sentence which needs more practice as it is not held so well in the auditive memory.

Feel the meaning

All drilling must be done with feeling. When the context is anger the teacher should clench their fists while modelling (speaking the pattern), then ask their students to do likewise while repeating. The same goes for all other gestures and body language that normally accompany speech. Some ELT handbooks ask the question, "Is one of the teacher's roles that of an actor?" I'll leave that up to you.

See the meaning

Sentences should be drilled only when there's total awareness of their meaning. Loss of consistent awareness can occur when a number of sentences in a dialogue or short narrative are being drilled. To prevent this you should have images available for screen sharing or pointing to; a quick drawing for each scene may be necessary at lower, especially mixed, levels. And of course your gestures and intonation would be essential.

Figure 7 Teacher gesturing 'emphatic statement of non-possession'. WB text includes intonation line and stress marking on final syllable.

At lower levels – self and whisper

When interacting with students there is plenty of opportunity for choral drilling, in fact drilling constitutes a great deal of beginner and elementary level teaching, as conversation is quite limited and the need for tackling pronunciation is great.

As a lead-in to a selection of short dialogues in the coursebook (which at lower levels you could design and write out yourself really, but the photos and attractive layout help with motivation) you could start with yourself and alternate with a few students, whispering the prompt and inviting with open hand for repetition and follow on. An example at beginner-elementary level follows; the objective is the present simple, clock times are roughly known already. (At the end I throw in an example of a quick explanation of the third person –s rule, the teacher aware that this rule is already known by the other students.):

> T: Monday, Tuesday, Wednesday, Thursday, every day, every day (writes *Every day* on WB). Every day I wake up, beep, beep, beep, beep (gestures with phone, opens eyes from sleeping mode, switches off phone, yawns and stretches. Draws bed and stickman – see figure 8). Who is this? Yes, it's me (students comment humorously). Every day I wake up at (writes *Every day I wake up at...*) Six? Seven? Eight?
> Ss: Six and half? Seven?
> T: Seven, correct, Kinzo. I wake up at seven o'clock (Draws speech balloon and writes/types within *I wake up at 7 o'clock every day* (adjusting/deleting the first *Every day*. Draws clock). Yes, I wake up at seven o'clock every day. (Groans) Oh, go to class, oh, terrible students! No, ha-ha, I love my students.

This section intentionally left blank.

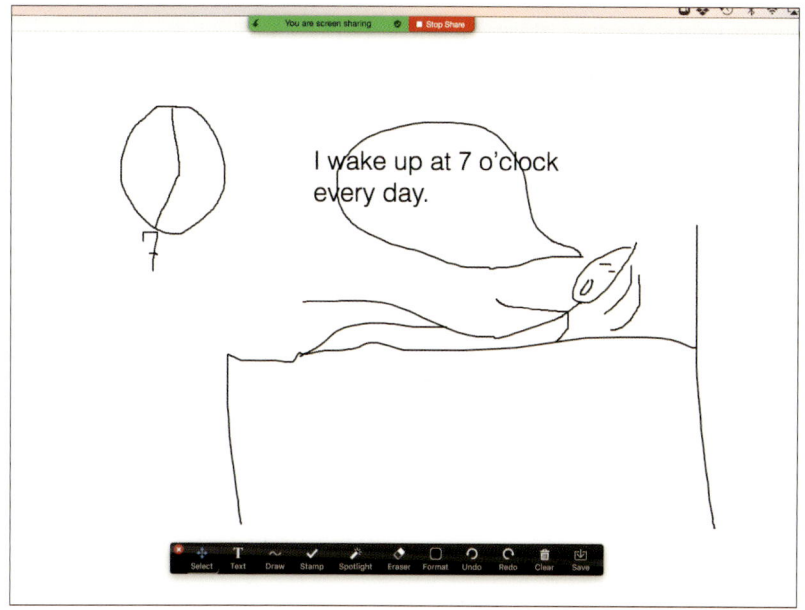

Figure 8 Drawing on the Zoom WB

() What time do you wake up, Felipe? What time (indicates watch/clock) do you (gestures) wake up?
F: I...
T: *(whispers)* I wake up at...
F: I wake up at... seven and half.
T: Good. Repeat, Felipe, I wake up at seven thirty (writes *7.30* on WB).
F: I wake up at seven thirty.
T: Thank you. (Writes *F. wakes up at 7.30 every day*.)
F: No Sunday.
T: Not on Sunday, never. But we say 'every day' for practice. Now (to all) listen: Felipe wakes up at 7.30 every day. Repeat.
Ss & T: Felipe wakes up at 7.30 every day.
T: Repeat.
Ss: Felipe wakes up at 7.30 every day.
T: *(After checking that 30 doesn't sound like 13)* Perfect, thank you. And (to all) be careful, don't call Felipe before 7:30.
S: Please, why 'wakes' not 'wake'?
T: I wake, you wake, he, she wakes. That's English.
S: Ok, thank you.

Using Drills in ELT 23

Instead of *7:30* above, I could have written *half past seven*, even *seven-thirty*, showing stress marking on *thírty*, but I just prefer numbers early on.

Teacher continues with one or two more students for *wake up* (+ choral drill) and moves on to *get up, have breakfast*, etc, followed by *What time does...* questions, according to the coursebook if using one.

WB work

Because the WB lends itself to drilling, especially at lower levels, some notes on its use have been added here.

Pad or mouse
Drawing on an online WB can be a little difficult but worth trying. A good tablet and stylus can help, especially for handwriting and including the schwa /ə/ at any size. However, just getting used to the mouse or trackpad will suffice for general use. Figures 8 and 9 were drawn with a mouse.

Keep phrases intact
In figure 8 'I wake up at' would have fit better in the top line, and 'seven o'clock every day' in the lower one. But language is learned in phrases, so it's best to retain the text in like manner, i.e. in this case, keep the preposition phrase 'at seven o'clock' intact. Don't present the language in a more difficult way than the way in which it is learned.

'I' on the WB is the writer; for drilling it's the students
When writing a sentence with 'I' on the WB the 'I' must refer to the person writing, mainly the teacher, obviously. In the above example, if Felipe had written on the WB he would have used 'I', but for choral drilling, the student's name will be the used. Don't choral drill 'I' unless it refers to all students, e.g. "I am learning English".

If you want to choral drill a sentence about yourself you should change the 'I' to your name or 'T' for the/our Teacher. The exception of course is when the text is in a speech balloon: then we can speak the line with 'I' as if role playing (indicate the text in the balloon when drilling).

Speech balloons
Speech balloons show instantly who is talking, and this is essential when two or more characters are involved. Try to put the first speaker and balloon on the left. The text doesn't have to fit neatly into the balloon.

Thought bubbles

These are good for showing and drilling conditionals, intentions, etc. The same advice concerning speech balloons applies. Example below.

Figure 9 A way of demonstrating and practising *I wish* + past perfect. Different colour font has been used for each student's offering.
Perfection is never important in WB drawing; in this one the doorway is crooked and I left it like that, the thought bubble could be bigger, etc.

Talk while drawing
Learning happens while you are drawing. Ask questions and pause, for example in figure 9 when the visitors are drawn first, ask "Where are they", then help with the door frame and door and speech balloon. Then draw the bottle of wine and ask, "Who are they?" (Parents, typically, but if students agree on 'friends', say that they are the fault-finding type). Then draw the daughter and ask if she looks happy (notice the line of her back). Ask "What is she thinking?" as you draw the thought bubble, then the grammar happens: drill your suggestion – *I wish I had known they were coming* – and elicit and drill the rest, and more – students can be very imaginative and creative!

The worse it is, the better it is
This is my maxim, having noted how students come to life when my drawing is deplorable, which it is – I never progressed from stick figures. Perfect sketches or downloaded images are lovely (ho-hum), but when you present your own effort your students are amused, and certainly engaged. Besides, you can't plan all your visual aids – be ready to welcome the unpredictable. Don't demur from drawing, you <u>can</u> do it.

Pre-inter level and higher
From pre-intermediate level onwards, more extensive T-S interaction is possible. During the lead-in stage of a lesson there are opportunities to choral drill lightly the patterns of the targeted language as they arise, especially if there are pronunciation difficulties. However, **most of the correction in the lead-in and pre-reading/listening stages is soft** (using recasting/reformulation). During the controlled practice stage, hard correction and drilling come to the fore. Please see the Appendix for an outline of these stages.

Soft corrrection and hard correction
An example of a **soft correction/ recasting/reformulation** would be:

> S: And the man fall
> T: Omigod! The man <u>fell</u>? He fell down? Really?
> S: Yes, he... f... fell.
> T: The poor man fell. And what did you do?

After a soft correction the student may or may not correct, it's up to them; the student above could have just replied "Yes" and that would be fine. In any case, the communication should continue without any noticeable break.

Soft correction, rather than none, which is often advised for T-S interaction, is also beneficial for the other students in the class who may be questioning the acceptability of the heard form, e.g. in the above case, whether the verb *fall* may be unchanged for the past tense.

An example of a **hard correction** would be:

> T: And now, number seven please, Hammad.
> S: Joe didn't mind… to work late that evening.
> T: Thanks Hammad. But it's: *Joe didn't mind working late.* After *mind* it's *–ing*, remember. You're a good student, you don't mind studying late. Well, yes, not too late. () So, is that ok?
> S: Yes, ok.
> T: Good. Repeat: Joe didn't mind working late.
> S: Joe didn't mind working late.
> T: Very good, thanks.

This example differs from the procedure in points 10-12 of *Controlled Practice* following, in that no other student has been first asked to suggest a correction. This is because we envisage here either a one-to-one class or the possibility that the teacher was under pressure of time.

When to choral drill

During controlled practice

The checking around part of the controlled practice stage (and when it suits, the checking around of the post reading questions) gives each student the opportunity of having at least one pronunciation difficulty ironed out. This is essential with multilingual groups, who would often have distinct phonological learning needs. The following two pages detail a typical controlled practice procedure. See the Appendix for lesson stages.

I recommend the use of coursebooks for general EL teaching. There is usually a good controlled practice stage in each lesson and in each lesson's workbook section, with the objective of consolidating the targeted language. Teachers may also find sections in a grammar practice book, e.g. Murphy (2019) that would fit their lesson.

Controlled Practice

Below is an updated version of 'Running through an exercise list' in Penston 2005, p12. (Any sentence/clause/phrase for drilling is not intended to have more than six stressed syllables.)
[Items in square brackets refer to online teaching alternatives.]

1 Show the page, point to and tap [highlight] the part in question. When all students are looking at that part nominate one to read the instructions – it saves your voice and gives the reader something extra to do while getting bonus pronunciation work – but don't nominate a student with excessively poor pronunciation.

2 If the first item, i.e. question/sentence (gap-fill, choice of correct form, etc.) is answered as an example, still have a good student read it aloud. This gives more time for the slower ones to understand what's required. If the first question is not done, do it yourself (Q & A with a good S) by way of example.

3 Initiate the collaborative pairwork. If some students prefer to work on their own that's fine.

4 While students work, make yourself available especially to the weaker ones, passing an eye over their work to check they are on the right track.

5 Assess whether it will be necessary to write the (correct) answers on the board as you receive them later. With vocab matching, true/false marking or multi-choice items there is usually no necessity; but where words or phrases have to be inserted or restructured then it's best to reinforce any oral confirmation of answers with board work. In advance, write question numbers and possibly some context, underline for blanks, etc.
[If screen-sharing a digital page/document, use Notation >> Text and other tools and type the answer as the S supplies it. Online/ebook teaching has a further advantage here: the correct multi-choice and other answers can be readily marked, giving visual confirmation.]

6 Start the check-around when most of the students have finished. The slower ones will understand that the whole class can't always wait on them; be sure to monitor them (don't nominate them) when you come to the last few questions. Start with a good student.

7 Usually, students should read out the full sentence to get pronunciation practice, not just say the missing word(s), or letter or number representing the missing word(s). This does not apply to reading comprehension multi-choice questions or similar.

8 Nominate with respect and clarity – call out the number of the next sentence and ask the student by name to attempt it. "Number three, Sung Yee please." is enough.

9 When you get a correct answer, say "Correct, thank you, X." and repeat the number and correct answer loudly. Check that all are ready for the next question (some may be erasing and correcting), then nominate the next student.

10 When you get a wrong answer don't just say "no". Thank the student by name but indicate there is a problem and ask if anybody got a different answer. Confirm or correct the peer correction, loudly and clearly, then once more repeat the number and the correct answer. By now the original student should have corrected their written answer, but if they still have difficulty you could do a quick explanation for them; this must be done briskly, the rest of the class are likely waiting to move on.

11 If an exercise involves a two-part dialogue, even of just two lines, have two students read it. We don't talk to ourselves in normal communication.

12 If a student's answer has a serious pronunciation error (one that could cause communication breakdown) or is too slow or broken, after confirming the correct answer *drill* it (individually):

Say "Listen", then model the correct phrase/clause (a full sentence is usually too long to drill). Then say "Repeat". If the sentence is on the WB point to [highlight] it, tapping out the rhythm and indicating any other phonetic aspects; besides helping visually this may reduce any anxiety for the student. If the student mispronounces again you should model again and do only one more *individual drill*. If you think the other students would benefit then *choral drill* once or twice as required.

13 Use your personality regarding the style of brief chit-chat that should occasionally arise along the way. Remember, if it were just a case of saying "next ... right ... next ... wrong," etc, then a robot would be better for this. But *you* can do what a robot can't: encourage, cajole, involve, personalize. The reasoning for this is to make the class more enjoyable and to provide consolidation, especially for slower students. It needn't be overdone, of course. Good teachers have quick examples ready when they spot an item not 'sitting in' well.

Sometimes the same student can be asked to do the next number also ("Because that one was too easy for you, Claudia."). It adds fun.

14 (Optional) When you've 'done' the section ask students to close their books, then review some of the items in a personalising style, i.e. elicit the same structure(s) but with relevant topics. This will not be possible with all exercises or all classes, and is easier to do in a one-to-one situation. However, it affords invaluable practice for the students and it will give you good training in effecting 'heads up' mode. An easier but still engaging activity is to say the first few words of each of the sentences and challenge the students to finish them from memory.

> **b** Underline the correct words to complete the sentences.
> 1 It's for girls only, so he *can / can't / has to* take part in the competition.
> 2 You really *can / ought to / don't have to* read this book about Jackie Chan. It's brilliant.
> 3 Louise *mustn't / doesn't have to / shouldn't* train hard because she is very talented.
> 4 You *mustn't / don't have to / are not allowed to* get nervous before the race.
> 5 The competition *was supposed / had / ought* to start at 7:00, but everyone was late.
> 6 Don't worry, you *mustn't / shouldn't / don't need to* train today.

Figure 10 From *Cambridge English Empower B2 Workbook* (W. Rimmer. Cambridge University Press 2015), usable as controlled practice. Errors to listen out for, even at this upper-intermediate level, would include the short rather than long vowel in *can't*, and *suppose-ed* rather than *suppozd*.

In other lesson stages

During the lead-in stage it is tempting to hard correct and drill errors, but soft correction (see page 26) is recommended in order to allow the 'chat' style of T-S interaction to flow. At the end of this stage and sometimes during it there is an opportunity to choral drill the targeted language presented (see the Appendix).

In the wrap-up stage any errors noted during the free practice would be corrected and the correct forms drilled. Targeted language would be reviewed, and drilled if required.

The stage least suitable for ending with a drill would be the pre-reading or pre-listening stage, where the movement towards the actual reading or listening would be better left unhindered.

Part of a dedicated pronunciation lesson

You might choose a number of sentences with particular phonologicial features for practice. Your coursebook would have dedicated pronunciation parts, normally in dialogue or other formats, and of course there are pronunciation practice materials online or in book + audio form.

It's best to mix other related activities into a 'pronunciation hour', such as dictation or dictogloss – primarily a listening skill activity where students can compare their work in pairs/groups before final checking.

Dictogloss (see Davis & Rinvolucri 1988, p70) is a form of dictation spoken at almost normal speed a number of times, followed by group collaboration for the final writing. You can see my effort on YouTube at
https://www.youtube.com/watch?v=XdjypWBrJgs&t=21s
and if you want to try that particular text, it and the teacher's notes are on pages 46-47.

Drilling a sentence on the WB

When a particular difficulty arises, the teacher may put the sentence on the WB. The procedure below is suggested for drilling a short sentence, clause or phrase, for any of which we use the word *sentence*, here and elsewhere. [Square brackets indicate notes for teaching online.]

1. Write/type the sentence on the WB. Remember that while writing you can elicit the final words and even the spelling of some of them, thereby keeping the students 'on board' if you'll pardon the pun.

2. Adjust the text where helpful, e.g. put an accent mark above the stressed syllables, put a slash mark through silent letters, put certain words together as one (e.g. *gas station > gasstation)*, use the schwa /ə/ if possible, draw a wavy line above the sentence to represent intonation, etc. Speak the sounds and allow repetition as you do these things, but don't drill.

3. Say "Listen"*, clearly and loudly, while looking directly at students for full attention.

4. Model (say clearly and loudly) the sentence. More than five or six stresses may be difficult to keep time to, so keep that as max.

5. While speaking, tap out the stressed syllables on your desk, [not too near your mic]. If intonation needs focus draw an intonation line over the sentence and say the sentence again while following the line with your pen.

6. Now say "Repeat"*. Tap out the stressed syllables again** while you repeat with the students. If helpful, conduct with your hand in the air (from right to left if showing intonation).

7. Again say 'Repeat'. This time don't repeat with the students. Listen for errors. Do this again if required***. [With online teaching choral drilling may not be feasible, depending on the technology. You may ask all students to repeat but in most cases you can only check a sample of the students individually.

8 If no difficulty is noted terminate the drill. If difficulty is noted with the majority of students model and drill one more time.

9 If difficulty is noted with one student, and this student would not suffer from being the focus of attention, nominate them, e.g. "Adriana, please listen and repeat." Thank them and confirm or correct (in a friendly manner). For correction you may just state the correct form loudly without referring to any phonological aspects, as by now it's time to move on.

10 Nominate one more student to produce the sentence. This can be one who just enjoys speaking or getting attention. Keep the customer happy.

* *Listen,* and *Repeat* are all that students need to hear. 'Ok' for 'listen' is ambiguous, and "Now, all together please" or similar is unnecessarily long. "Listen and Repeat" (followed by the model sentence) would also work, but only when the students are used to your style and you deliver the line prominently.
**If intonation is to be practised, follow the intonation line instead of tapping the stressed syllables.
*** If you're asking, "Required by whom?" the answer must be, "By the students, assessed/consulted by the teacher."

A daily pronunciation routine

You can start each day with a proverb or a short quotation. You can first ask students if there is a proverb in their own language similar to the one you will elicit, for example one which means, 'You should respect others' cultures'. Then write *When in Rome, do as the Romans do,* and drill. You can elicit the previous day's proverb and have an end-of-week quiz, e.g. asking what proverb gives such and such advice, or giving the first few words as prompts. As with a lot of online quiz answering, students may write their answers in the chat panel; first correct one wins.

Figure 11 Example of a proverb used for a drill, showing typical phonological features: final consonant transition onto following word, stress marking (with accent), schwa /ə/ in weak forms, intonation line. The schwa is written small to indicate its weak quality. The intonation line in this case is only considered necessary on the last word.

For review
Drilling should never become disagreeable – if fluency in a pattern can't be achieved today leave it for another day. Put it on your list of quick fillers as a review. When revisited, the reaction can be quite different, especially when the task is set as a challenge ("We can do this").

Other activities
1. Short (gap-fill) dialogues
Most coursebooks up to intermediate level will have short dialogues for listening, some with the script in the main body of the lesson for oral work also, often with gaps. You can write dialogues yourself too, of course, targeting specific language areas. Below is a suggestion for their exploitation. (*Sentence* = short sentence, clause or phrase.)

> 1 Do the normal pre-listening work (set the scene, show image of the speakers, etc.). For lower levels especially, ensure that the students know which character talks first by reading out their line as you point to or highlight them.
>
> 2 Play the audio through, with dialogue text masked, but with coursebook images or drawn ones on show (I admit I sometimes also show the dialogue text during the first listening, it depends on the class and the text).
>
> 3 Students now look at the dialogue text.
>
> *If there is gap-fill:*
>
> 3a Play a second time, pausing after each gap and allowing for filling in. Elicit and confirm the answer. Replay the completed phrase if required.
>
> Continue from 3b.
>
> *If there isn't gap-fill:*
>
> 3b Play the audio again, pausing after each sentence and choral drilling it. This may not be necessary for all sentences – you will know which ones present no difficulty and are better passed over. If serious pronunciation is noted, drill the sentence a second time (model the line yourself, emphasizing the part for attention). No individual checking or boardwork is done here.
>
> With a list of sentences like this there's obviously no need to repeat the "listen" instruction; the "repeat" one would also be greatly reduced as the students follow the procedure.

3c You may drill with one side of the class for each character, then swap and drill again (further breakup for three or more characters may be feasible). This takes longer but it is closer to normal interaction and is generally preferred.

4 Depending on student need, play and drill again in like manner, speeding up the repetition.

5a Have students role-play (read) the parts in pairs or small groups, depending on the number of characters. Insist on good intonation; give a couple of examples, emphasising important points.

5b Students swap/rotate roles and read their lines again.

6 (Optional) Students do the same but in a 'look, cover, then speak' method (not reading aloud directly).

7 If you hear a persistent error, use the board to highlight relevant phonetic aspects, choral drill twice, and finish.

A **[12.2] Listen and read.** What's Ming going to do for the charity dance? Then repeat the conversation and replace the words in **bold**.

REAL ENGLISH Definitely!

Nadine: We're going to have the charity dance in the gym. Who's going to decorate it?

Ming: I am! I **made some awesome decorations**. (**made some cool posters** / **bought lots of balloons**)

Nadine: OK, we need music. Maya, are you going to be the DJ?

Maya: Definitely! I'm going to play some cool **hip-hop** music. (**rock** / **dance**)

Nadine: Who's going to bring the food?

Stig: I'm going to **bake some cookies**. Ming's going to help. (**make cupcakes** / **bake a cake**)

Ming: So, Nadine, what are you going to do?

Nadine: Well, I'm going to come to the dance and **eat the cookies!** (**have a great time** / **enjoy the music**)

Figure 12 From *Time Zones 2* (National Geographic Learning, 2020). Dialogue with substitution words, which ensures that students will read the dialogue at least twice after listening.

2. Video

Films

We shan't go into detail on how to exploit films for classroom learning; there are discussion groups on the internet that serve well for such matters. However, we do advise that subtitling be available with whatever you intend using, and that it be used according to students' wishes. You will probably show a segment of the film at regular periods, perhaps each week. During that showing you could pause the video a number of times (not as much as would spoil the enjoyment of the film), and cue a drilling of the important sentence visible on the subtitle line, or brought up on the line if you had suppressed the subtitling. Just two choral repetitions is advised, then move on.

Coursebook clips

Most coursebooks now come with a video component, mainly consisting of short scenes or interviews. Some subtitling may be set in about four lines, with the spoken line highlighted; this allows the students to see the line in more context. You may pause on any line and drill it if required; this is done usually on the second showing (you may have done the first showing without subtitles).

Shorts

Film shorts are also available online and are a good choice when an easy learning option is called for; several come with lesson plans.

3. Poetry

Poems are written to be read aloud and usually have a rhythm that can be shown and enjoyed. Unfortunately, being authentic material they make little concession for language learners, hence I don't recommend their use below a strong intermediate level. Choose a poet that is well known or otherwise of interest as this ensures higher motivation. Short and manageable poems are best.

A poem about a choice

Robert Frost's *The Road Not Taken* is widely known and liked, perhaps because we can all recollect a moment when we had to decide on a course in life, or maybe just a path in a park, when the decision seemed to hold some importance or led to an important event. This is one of those topics that engages students from the start.

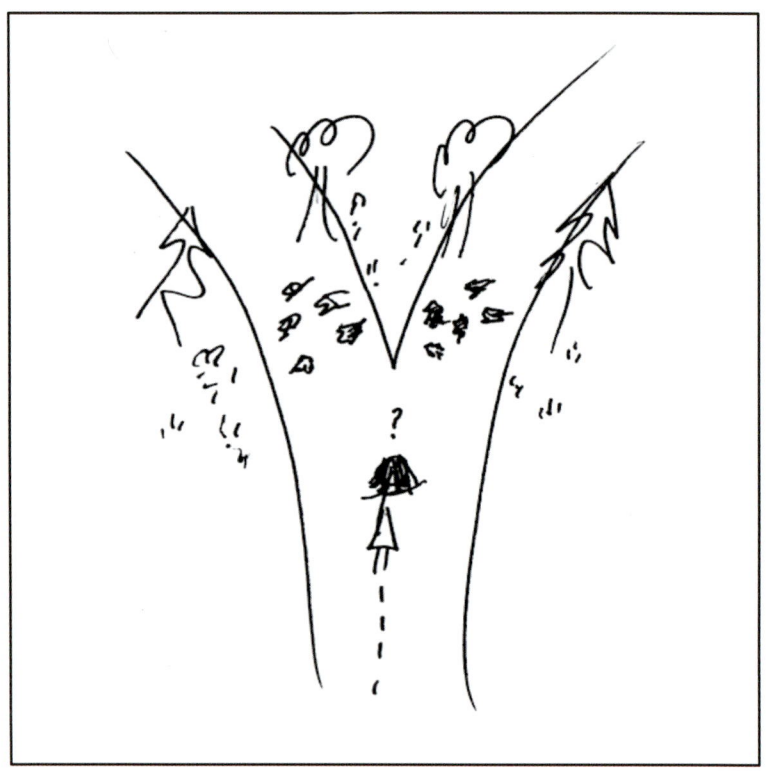

Figure 13 Board drawing doable in less than half a minute. More detail can be added as you talk. This is much faster and more fun than downloading images.

Method

1 Lead-in and pre-teach in the normal way: elicit how we make choices when there's not much between the options (mention how you did/ almost did something big). Show/draw (and elicit) <u>a wood</u>, <u>undergrowth</u>, <u>leaves</u> (what colour is a wood?); tread on some realia, e.g. wadded paper, to include <u>trodden</u>; show paths <u>diverging</u>, ask students how they would know the better path, ask which is <u>worn</u>, which has more <u>wear</u>; ask which path they would take and why. Which did the poet take (prediction question)? Elicit how making a small choice can influence the rest of one's life. You could ask pairs to chat for a couple of minutes, comparing choices they have made in their lives.

THE ROAD NOT TAKEN by Robert Frost (1874-1963)

Two roads diverged in a yellow wood
And sorry I could not travel both
And be one traveler, long I stood
And looked down one as far as I could
To where it bent in the undergrowth;

Then took the other, as just as fair
And having perhaps the better claim,
Because it was grassy and wanted wear;
Though as for that, the passing there
Had worn them really about the same,

And both that morning equally lay
In leaves no step had trodden black.
Oh, I kept the first for another day!
Yet knowing how way leads on to way,
I doubted if I should ever come back.

I shall be telling this with a sigh
Somewhere ages and ages hence:
Two roads diverged in a wood and I —
I took the one less traveled by,
And that has made all the difference.

2 If teaching online I prefer students to have printed out the poem rather than rely solely on the screen, because some like to add translations and pronunciation marks.
Tell students to read the poem quietly. Answer any questions on vocabulary. There may be a question on the grammaticality of *as just as fair*, which would be explained as an example of poetic licence. Grammatically correct options would be *As it was just as fair* or *it being just as fair*, but either of these may have stretched the iambus too far for Frost's liking. Of course, this kind of poetry analysis is best left to students of literature – ELT students and teachers have more fun and just enjoy the poems!
3 Read the whole poem aloud.
4 Ask students if they think Frost was happy about his choice in the end.

5 Drill the first stanza line by line with the whole class. You may think this won't work but students who want to improve their fluency will readily cooperate. Don't redrill in the case of any errors as this breaks the momentum.
6 Carry on likewise with the other stanzas. Make a mental note of some of the more serious errors.
7 Elicit any further comments.
8 Deal with two or three serious mispronunciations on the board, showing any relevant phonological properties.
9 Free Practice: ask students to write three or four sentences about a choice they made and the resulting situation, real or invented. Monitor and fix some errors. Students in groups of three share (read aloud) their work and guess the veracity of each. Move a member from each group to share again with the next group (rotate) if time allows.
10 Revert to the poem: read a stanza aloud and invite a S to read it after you (one stanza per student). Correct only one mispronunciation per S. When all the stanzas are done but more students want a go and the class is amenable, oblige. If a S with very poor pronunciation wants to try a stanza, let them repeat line by line after you, with no corrections.

4. Jazz chants

The term Jazz Chants® was invented by Carolyn Graham in the US, whose books of chants are still quite popular. Jazz chants are generally a form of fun poetry, usually to be accompanied by clapping in time on the stressed syllables. Most are or can be adapted as two-part dialogues, which makes for good 'two halves of class' choral chanting. Here's one I wrote myself, stresses marked with accents:

A: *Have you gót my péncil?* B: *Nó, not mé*
A: *Did Áhmed táke it?* B: *Nó, not hé. Hé's got twó. He dóesn't need thrée.*
A: *Whát'll I dó?* B: *You can bórrow míne.*
A: *Is thát okáy?* B: *Súre, it's fíne.*
A: *Yóu're a pál.* B: *Évery tíme.*

Clapping on the stresses

In *he dóesn't need thrée* in B above, there are technically three stresses, but the tone grouping allows for a reduction to two.

Try a jazz chant with your class. As long as there's regular rhythm echoing from one side of the class to the other, where each half can enjoy clapping on the stresses, or tapping if this is preferable, then the objective – feeling and learning the rhythm of English – has been achieved. Here's one that's certainly for young learners. There are four beats to each line.

A	B
Dínosáurs are réally cóol	Í prefér my bóoks in schóol
Thís one's góing to éat a mán	Thát was nót póssible thén
Look óut! Here cómes a stégosáur	A stégosáurus, véry bórus
Hére's T-Réx, he'll éat you úp	Gíve him a drínk from a páper cúp.

Realia of toy dinosaurs is almost essential here – it would be a shame to have learners say "this one" while holding nothing (this applies for all role plays). Cardboard cutouts would suffice, with optional colouring time included in the lesson. Note the opportunity for supercilious intonation (falling) with **B**'s lines. **B**'s last line doesn't really follow, but often that kind of semi-nonsense is child-friendly. **B** can have some fun with body language, demonstrated by the teacher.

Although most jazz chants are for children, they can also work well with adults who like to let their hair down occasionally. Here's one for business people:

A	B
The Dów Jónes is dówn agáin	The DÁX, tóo, nóthing néw
Emérging márkets dídn't shíne	I álways trústed Éastern mínes
Áviátion's táking óff	It's wórth a trý, but the rísk is hígh
Commódities are wórth a shót	Gréen énergy's álways hót
RÓI on rýe is hígh	Whískey? Nó thanks, Í'll stay drý.

Method

1 Pre-teach any difficult vocabulary or concept, otherwise go straight to the action, but do use visuals and props where helpful.
2 Show the text on the board or screen with primary stress marks (accent marks will do).
3 Read the text aloud, tapping on the stressed syllables. Use a different tone of voice for **A** and **B**.
4 Divide the class into two sides.
5 Drill each question and retort line-by-line for the appropriate sides of the class, tapping on the stressed syllables.

6 Drill again, clapping on the stressed syllables, students to clap with you.
7 Repeat the drill with clapping.
8 Swap roles and drill again, clapping.

Don't forget to return to the same jazz chant or poem or song at a later date. The rhythm of English is perhaps the hardest thing to acquire and students should enjoy noticing their progress with it.

5. Songs

Songs are not for drilling, but if learners are encouraged to sing along after the usual listening task, this is repetition. Even the listeners are engaging in a form of repetition, the benefits of which have been stated on page 16. So, songs are one of the most effective learning instruments and should be used well and often. Don't forget to return to a song again, and maybe again. How many times have you heard the same song?

6. Limericks

Limericks can be fun. They're short and snappy and therefore easy to drill. Here's one:

There once was a man from Devizes
Whose ears came in two different _____
One was too small
It was no good __ ___
But the other won several _____ .

Method

1 Explain the rhyming scheme. If you have the facility you can quickly show a prepared example, e.g.

> There was a young lady from Riger,
> Who smiled as she rode on a tiger.
> They returned from the ride
> With the lady inside
> And a smile on the face of the tiger.

2 Write/show the main limerick with stress marks and some rhyming words missing. It's better to write, because then you can easily and quickly show phonological points by substituting the schwa, changing the size of letters, crossing/rubbing out silent letters, putting words together, stretching out syllables, etc.

3 Read the limerick through, exaggerating the stressed vowels, and pausing at each blank.
4 Now elicit the missing words, helping with rhyming sounds.
5 Choral drill line by line, tapping on the stressed syllables.
6 Drill again, checking for typical pronunciation errors such as poor linkages and strong pronunciation of weak vowels.
7. Choral drill the whole limerick line by line one last time.
   You can see my effort at
   https://www.youtube.com/watch?v=OljS6mjxSt4

Poetic pronunciation licence applies in the first line of limericks where the verb *be* is stressed, e.g. *There wás a young mán from Perú*. I doubt if this causes a carry-over into learner speech, but you should perhaps clarify the matter whenever it arises.

7. Disappearing text

This involves drilling a short text, line by line or clause by clause, then deleting/erasing a small number of words and asking students to read all, filling in the blanks from memory. Choral drill the line if any mistake or mispronunciation occurs. Then delete more and carry on until all the words are deleted or the fun in the challenge flags.

Suitable texts would be part of a lesson you have recently covered, a short piece of news, a verse of a poem or song (not too well known).

Can you remember the missing words in Frost's poem?

```
I shall be _____ this with a sigh
Somewhere _____ and _____ hence:
_____ roads _____ in a wood and I —
I took the one _____ traveled by,
And _____ has _____ ____ the difference.
```

To add more fun you could split the class into two teams. Each team takes its turn to read a consecutive line. If there is a delay or mistake the other team steals the chance to say the line properly and win a point.

The two-team idea can work for dialogues too. Below is an imagined dialogue between Rosa Parks, the civil rights activist, and the bus driver. Two or more words together can be erased when they occur in tight collocation – you can leave two blanks or one for this, depending on your class level. I've already erased a few words to start you off. They are deducible from context. Answers follow.

> You _____ sit in the front seats. They're for whites.
> Can I _____ in the middle seats?
> Only if no _____ need them.
> Ok, there's plenty of _____ seats for them.
> ....
> Now all the front seats are _____. All blacks vacate the middle seats.
> But then we'll _____ __ stand. That ain't fair.
> Tough luck! You know the law. Stop wastin' my _____.
> I ain't movin'. I'm _____ a stand, sittin' down. I'm tired of this segregation stuff.
> If you carry on _____ _____ you're gonna be arrested.
> I guess you're gonna have to have me arrested, _____.
>
> Answers:
> can't, sit, whites, front, full, have to, time, makin'/(takin'), like that/this, then/(so).

The above dialogue generates fun with intonation and accents. Points to look out for would include the difference between *can't* and *can* (/kɑːnt/ and /kən/) the different stresses between the first and second *them*, stress pattern on *you know the law*, and the voiceless and voiced final consonant in the consecutive *have*'s in the last line.

8. Chaining

Chaining is where a sentence goes from student to student, changing a little on its way, e.g. the *I went to the shop/store and I bought...* game, where the next student repeats the sentence and adds on another product. Penalty points may be incurred for forgotten items or delays.

Similar chaining games include *Bringing to the Party*. The T starts off by saying "I'm going to the party and I'm bringing/ going to bring balloons". The T's name is Belinda, and B is the first letter of her name and of 'balloons', so she can go. If a S says, "I'm going to the party and I'm going to bring pasta," but the S's name doesn't begin with a P then the T says they can't come. This does the rounds until a number of students discover the secret. Etc.

Concentric Circles (students A inner, students B outer) is another method of having Ss repeat, this time the same Q & A (e.g. 'speed dating', personal info). After each exchange one circle moves to make a new S-S pairing. For online teaching, breakout rooms would suffice.

These chaining games and similar would be regarded as semi-controlled or semi-free practice, and the only drilling to take place would be during the setting up of the activity and in correcting any serious errors.

9. Role-play

I'm including role-play here because it actually involves drilling. Intonation, stress, timing, all are crucial for successful drama, and the teacher needs to help with these, drilling the lines, when circulating to rehearse each actor. Hopefully your students will eventually perform, to the class or school, or just record the video for their parents or friends; but remember that no one likes to hear lines delivered in monotone. Browse and select a book of role plays suitable for your students' age group and level, or write your own.

The following sketch is based on an old joke, retold in *Fun Class Activities* by P. Watcyn-Jones. Penguin, 2000. It requires lots of exaggeration of intonation, pauses, facial expressions. Without these it will lose a lot of its effect and enjoyment. Drill during rehearsals.

Two women, or a woman and man, seated. Watcyn-Jones has added that they're feeding ducks, in which case have props (small pieces of wadded paper) and someone to make the occasional quacking noise. The ellipses with 'Oh', 'Yes', and 'Er' indicate a mild double take.
Pre-teach poisoned mushrooms, coincidence, skull.

A: Ah yes. I've had three husbands, and they're all dead now.
B: What? All of them? That's so sad. How unfortunate.
A: Yes, all of them. One, two, three. Two was the hardest, a strong fella!
B: … Oh. … But, what happened? How did they die?
A: Well, Billy, the first husband, he died of eating poisoned mushrooms.
B: Poisoned mushrooms! Well, yes, you do have to be careful with mushrooms.
A: You sure do. And we'd only been married a year.
B: Only a year! That's terrible! … And how did the second one die?
A: Well, this is hard to believe, I know, but the second one went the same way.
B: Poisoned mushrooms??
A: Exactly. And we'd only been married a year.
B: What? What a coincidence! What a terrible coincidence!
A: Dead right.
B: … Yes. …   It goes to show how dangerous mushrooms can be, doesn't it?
A: It certainly does. They're very effective.
B: … Er… yes. You've had some bad luck alright. … And the third one?
A: Poor Cedric. He died of a broken skull.
B: What! A broken skull? Oh dear! Was he in an accident?
A: No, I hit him on the head with a baseball bat.
B: You hit him on the head with a baseball bat!? But why?
A: Well… he wouldn't eat his mushrooms!

Frequency of repetition

The attainment of language fluency is not knowledge-dependent. Rules and lexis can be learnt, but fluency can only be achieved through repetition. How much repetition is the learner's prerogative. In this book, the number of times a pattern is directed to be repeated is to be taken as suggested. With experience you will 'feel' how much of any activity your students need and want. Or they will tell you.

Conclusion and outlook

Language teaching and learning has come a long way from meaningless repetition in a teacher-led environment to, hopefully, meaningful repetition in a learner-centred environment. Technological aspects, too, have made great strides, and learners can use their phones or other devices to get accurate feedback on their pronunciation.

Despite the attraction and affordability of app and web lessons, many learners still prefer to interact with a human, and in a physical classroom if possible. However, many factors favour online teaching. Individual drilling is well catered for online, but choral drilling is only possible if the technology for syncing audio and video is available and is availed of. With adult learners this may be the norm, but with a class of teenagers or young learners more time may be needed for the syncing to function across their different devices.

As long as the teacher knows the value of drilling and knows how to drill, learners will be happy, especially those whose L1 differs greatly from English.

Finally, for any reader who may still doubt the efficacy of drilling, let me cite the results of classroom research carried out over a 10-week period in Kyiv (Parfitt & Reid 2019), where for five minutes in each lesson 'standard repetition' (the simple repetition advocated here) was used in one class (Class 1), and in two other classes (Classes 2 and 3) either 'chaining' or 'Chinese whispers' or no repetition was used.

Pre- and post period testing yielded the following results in pronunciation skills:

Global improvement in scores:
Class 1: 71%
Classes 2 & 3: 33%

Appendix
Lesson plan format

Below is a greatly reduced version of the popular lesson plan format known as PPP (**P**resentation, i.e. reading/listening/oral input; **P**ractice, i.e. controlled practice; **P**roduction, i.e. free practice).

Re terminology, some training tutors use *lexis* instead of *vocabulary*.

STAGE	ACTIVITY
LEAD-IN	Introductions and warm-up. If first lesson of the day check any homework. Interact with Ss, leading to the topic of the lesson. Elicit/feed some relevant vocabulary. Put an example of targeted language on the WB, and drill lightly (without insisting on perfection).
PRE-READING/ LISTENING	Build interest in the topic. Pre-teach some of the new vocab using the context of a similar topic (and visuals). Elicit some predictions. Direct Ss to any pre-reading questions in the coursebook.
READING/ LISTENING	Ss read text / listen to audio (& watch video). Ss answer pre- and post reading questions in their coursebook. Some of the latter can be treated as controlled practice if appropriate (drill if required).
CONTROLLED PRACTICE	Grammar points and vocab met in the reading/listening are practised, usually from an exercise list. Nominate around, correct any errors and drill where required. (See p29.)
FREE/FREER PRACTICE	Ss take part in an activity which is relatively free from T participation and normally practises the targeted language of the lesson, overtly or otherwise. The activity can be a language game, pair work interview, pair work info-gap, role play, mingling Q & A, group discussion, etc. Online research may be included, especially for project work.
WRAP-UP	Show on the WB any errors noted during free practice and elicit correct forms. Drill these if required. Review targeted language. Thank Ss. If last lesson of the day assign any homework. Lesson ends.

DICTOGLOSS – *THE CLADDAGH RING* – TEACHER'S NOTES
(See page 31)

- Draw or show a Claddagh ring.
- Pre teach *Claddagh*, now a suburb of Galway (show map), *Richard Joyce* for spelling; *goldsmith, craftsman*. And for lower levels, *slave, precious*.
- Check understanding of 'Ground Zero'.

- Read out the first paragraph/section three times at careful but not slow speed. First, no pens, then on the second and third time notes may be made.
- Ss in groups of three compare notes and reconstruct what they've heard.
- When all or most have finished, carry on with the next paragraphs.

When finished dictating:
1. If using technology, Ss upload their work via their phones for all to compare.
2. Ss read each work and groups agree marks for others' content and clarity.
3. If no devices are in use, have groups mount their work on the walls. Ss read each and groups agree marks for others' content and clarity. And/or have groups reconstruct a summary, with maximum two sentences per paragraph. Ask a S from each group to come to the front and present their summary. (Make notes of good points, and any serious errors, which can be covered later.)
4. Assess/adjust marks given. Add marks for presentation skills if pertinent.
5. Distribute/show the dictated text (on the next page).

Background to the story:
According to legend, shortly before he was due to be married, a fisherman named Richard Joyce, from Claddagh in Galway, was captured by pirates and sold as a slave in Algeria. He became the property of a rich goldsmith, who trained him in his craft. In time, Richard became a fully proficient craftsman and, with thoughts of his fiancée close to his heart, he made the first Claddagh ring.

The heart symbolizes love, the hands symbolize security and friendship, and the crown is for loyalty and fidelity. The heart can be a precious stone, usually an emerald, or silver or gold like the ring itself.

After some years Joyce was freed, and on his return he found that his sweetheart had waited for him, and, presenting her with the Claddagh ring they were married.

The secret of the Claddagh is how you wear it. If the point of the heart is turned outwards this means your heart is unoccupied. If the heart is facing inwards this means you have a lover.

The design has become so popular it has been extended to earrings, brooches, pendants, etc.

In October 2001 the Irish foreign minister visited Ground Zero. When he met the Chief of the NYPD he asked him if he had found a Claddagh ring in the wreckage, because the Irish parents of one of the missing firefighters said he always wore it. "Minister," the chief said, "we have found 200 Claddagh rings."

(*Irish Times*, October 2001)

DICTOGLOSS – *THE CLADDAGH RING* – TEXT FOR DICTATION

There is a deliberate double space after each full stop to indicate a short pause.

THE CLADDAGH RING

A fisherman named Richard Joyce from Claddagh, near Galway, was captured by pirates and sold as a slave in Algeria. There, he became the property of a rich goldsmith. In time, Richard became a good craftsman and, thinking of his fiancée, he made the first Claddagh ring.

The heart symbolizes love, the hands symbolize security, and the crown is for loyalty. The heart can be a precious stone, usually an emerald, or silver or gold.
After some years Joyce was freed, and on his return he presented the ring to his sweetheart and they were married.

The secret of the Claddagh is how you wear it. If the point of the heart is turned outwards this means your heart is unoccupied. If the heart is facing inwards this means you have a lover.

At Ground Zero in New York two hundred Claddagh rings were found.

Bibliography

Baker, A. (2006) *Ship or Sheep*. Cambridge University Press.
Brooks, N. (1964) *Language and Language Learning: Theory and Practice*. Harcourt Brace.
Collier Macmillan (1978) *New English 900, Book 4*. Macmillan.
Davis, P, & Rinvolucri, M. (1988) *Dictation – New Methods and Possibilities*. Cambridge University Press.
Ehrenman, G. (2004) Split Decision. *Mechanical Engineering-CIME*, 126/12, p22. *Gale Academic OneFile*. Accessed 18 Sept. 2020.
Ellis, N.C. (2002) Frequency effects in language processing. *Studies in Second Language Acquisition* 24/2, 143-188.
ESMA Montreal (2015) *Tea Time* film short. Accessible on YouTube.
Hancock, M. (2017) *Pronpack 3*. Hancock McDonald ELT.
Larsen-Freeman, D. (1986) *Techniques and Principles in Language Teaching*. Oxford University Press.
Lewis, M. (1993) *The Lexical Approach*. Cengage.
Littlewood, W. (1981) *Communicative Language Teaching: An Introduction*. Cambridge University Press.
Moody, K.W. & Gibbs, P.H. (1967) *Teaching Structures in Situations*. African Universities Press in association with The British Council.
Murphy, E (2012) https://abcnews.go.com/blogs/entertainment/2012/11/nicole-westbrook-goes-viral-with-its-thanksgiving-song-video
Murphy, R. (2019) *English Grammar in Use, 5th ed*. Cambridge University Press.
Parfitt, R. & Reid, C. (2019) To drill or not to drill. *English Teaching Professional* 122, 8-10
Peachey, N. (2020) *Tea Time* – video shorts lesson plan (see ESMA above). Peachey Publications.
Penston, T. (2005) *A Concise Grammar for English Language Teachers*. TP Publications.
Penston, T. (2015) *Essential Phonetics for English Language Teachers*. TP Publications.
Richards, J. & Rodgers, T. (1986) *Approaches and Methods in Language Teaching*. Cambridge University Press.
Skinner, B.F. (1957) *Verbal behavior*. Appleton.
Stevick, E. (1976) *Memory, Meaning and Method*. Heinle & Heinle.
Thomson, A.J. & Martinet, A.V. (1979) *Structure Drills 2*. Oxford University Press.
Underhill, A. (2018a) Grammar without pron is like food without taste. *Modern English Teacher* 27/1, 4-7.
Underhill, A. (2018b) Grammar without pron is like food without taste (Part 2). *Modern English Teacher* 27/2, 53-56.
Van Ek, J. & Alexander, L.G. (1977) *The Threshold Level for Modern Language Learning in Schools*. Longman.
Widdowson, H.G. (1978) *Teaching Language as Communication*. Oxford University Press.